A POET TO
AND TO TU
AND AGAIN . . .

# ROD McKUEN

"The example par excellence of a man who has not only understood freedom for himself but for all the others for whom he writes and sings. The result is honesty—not just of his poetry, but of the man."
—*Los Angeles Herald-Examiner*

Enter now the special world of Rod McKuen as he celebrates life and loving in warm and poignant verse and photographs.

A Biplane Book

# Hand in Hand...

A KANGAROO BOOK
PUBLISHED BY POCKET BOOKS NEW YORK

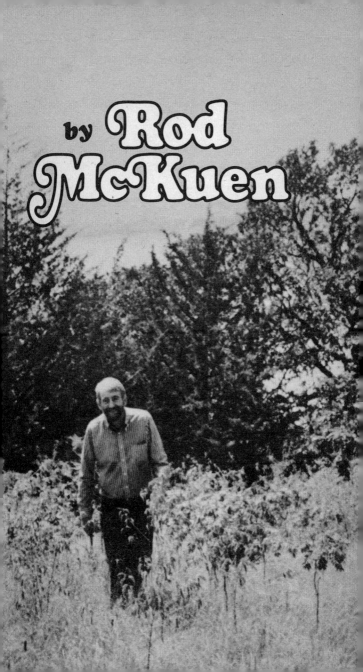

by **Rod McKuen**

# A Biplane Book

## HAND IN HAND

POCKET BOOK edition published May, 1977

In addition to the books listed in the Sources section, some of the poems in this collection have appeared in *The New York Times, Folio, Woman's Day, Saturday Review, The Christian Science Monitor, The London Daily Express, T.V. Times,* and *Poetry Review.*

This original POCKET BOOK edition is printed from brand-new plates made from newly set, clear, easy-to-read type.
POCKET BOOK editions are published by
POCKET BOOKS,
a Simon & Schuster Division of
GULF & WESTERN CORPORATION
1230 Avenue of the Americas,
New York, N.Y. 10020.
Trademarks registered in the United States
and other countries.

ISBN: 0-671-81045-6.

1287

Cover and art direction by Hy Fujita.

Photography by Hy Fujita, Rod McKuen, David Nutter, and Wayne Massie.

Coordinator for BIPLANE BOOKS: Wade Alexander

Printed in the U.S.A.

This is a book for L.D.S.
Being alive is the best part of living.

# Books by Rod McKuen

## *Prose*

Finding My Father
In His Own Words

## *Poetry*

And Autumn Came
Stanyan Street & Other Sorrows
Listen to the Warm
Lonesome Cities
In Someone's Shadow
Caught in the Quiet
Fields of Wonder
And to Each Season
Come to Me in Silence
Moment to Moment
Celebrations of the Heart
Beyond the Boardwalk
*The Sea Around Me, The Hills Above

## *Collected Poems*

Twelve Years of Christmas
A Man Alone
With Love . . .
The Carols of Christmas
Seasons in the Sun
Alone
*The Rod McKuen Omnibus
Hand in Hand

_____

*Available only in Great Britain.

## Collected Lyrics

New Ballads
Pastorale
The Songs of Rod McKuen
Grand Tour

## Music Collections

The Annotated Rod McKuen Song Book
The McKuen/Sinatra Song Book
New Ballads
At Carnegie Hall
McKuen/Brel: Collaboration
28 Greatest Hits
Jean and Other Nice Things
McKuen Country
New European Windows
Greatest Hits, Vol. I
Greatest Hits, Vol. II
Children's Song Book

## Classical Music

Concerto for Cello & Orchestra
Symphony #1
The Plains of My Country
Six Piano Studies
The City
Concerto for Piano & Orchestra
Symphony #3

## Opera

The Black Eagle

# Author's Note

The sound of one hand clapping, while admittedly a sometimes joyful noise, is so lonesome as to leave no echo in its wake. And while we *come into the world alone and go away the same,* life is somehow made easier with the joining of hands. Body contact says it all: in a handshake; an arm about the shoulder; a tentative, reaching, nighttime touch across a room or the wide space of a mattress; even hand-to-hand combat done on foreign or friendly soil.

This is a book about reaching, extending not only a hand or arm toward another, but toward the unknown, the faces only conjured, invisible things, the stars, sometimes even God. Most of what is here goes beyond the reaching stage toward stability; hence, the title *Hand in Hand*.

I do not consider this "collection poetry" in a formal sense. No apology, more a whispered boast. While part of me thought I was writing poems, another part knew I was setting down communiqués. No messages are sent but those we send to one another. These words, and strung-together words, still stay private. They are between *us*.

*From me to you.*
The simplicity of that sentence is what poetry,
even communication, should be about.

Rod McKuen

California, 1977


The poetry contained in this volume has been selected from material written over the past twenty-two years. Dedications of individual chapters seldom have anything to do with the poems contained therein (some will observe that many of these same poems were written for and dedicated to others throughout the year).

Names, therefore, are further hand signals to friends—semaphores to let them know that for some particular reason, most often my own neglect, I'm thinking of them.

# Contents

# *Preamble*

I need nothing
    when you're gone
        but you.

—from *Beyond the Boardwalk*

## Creed

It doesn't matter
who you love
or how you love
but *that* you love.

For in the end
the act of loving any man.
is the act of loving God.

The good in men
is all the God there is
and loving is a contribution
to that good
and to that only God.

## Atlas

Don't be afraid
to fall asleep with gypsies
        or run with leopards.
As travelers or highwaymen
we should employ
whatever kind of wheels it takes
to make our lives
go smoothly down the road.

And if you love somebody
                tell them.
Love's a better road map
for trucking down the years
than Rand McNally ever made.

## Invocation

I do not doubt
that in some hidden
             middle night
you'll rise up
and come to me
in solitude or silence.

We will meet
as we have met
on a train or at the end
of some new train of thought.

# Two By Two

for Lou Thomas

Run or fly
comes in circles
if you must.
Ovals that do not
          turn back.

—from *Beyond the Boardwalk*

## Spaces

Spaces there are
that won't be filled
not by remembering
            or reaching.
Sometimes the distance
separating those who love
lies between them
in the same small bed.
And though the separation
                is but inches
it might as well be miles.

Distance is distance
and holding one the other
                    close
is arm's length all the same.

# February Morning, 2

We cannot close the cold out
not if it's within ourselves.
Nor can we keep the fire
            burning always
however carefully
the fire's been set.

Love, then,
while the candle lives.
Don't look ahead
            and wonder
who, if anyone,
            will snuff it out.

# Worry

Blinking like an owl
            in morning,
I woke up wanting you
   for all the Denver days ahead
               and ever after.
For all the Sausalitos past
and Boston nights that ended
before they had beginnings.

Thick-throated still
and not yet
           wide awake enough
I finally came alive
to find you studying me.

I wish that I
had told you then
I wasn't what you watched,
and given time to rearrange
my face and frame for you,
I'd be closer to the man
who picked you up
            the night before.
Nearer to whatever
you must have wanted
or expected.

But seeing you
at my breath's edge
filled my head
with such a wonder
that I could only
pray in silence
that though your eyes
            were open
you stared at me from sleep.
A sleep I wouldn't dare
                invade.

## Excelsior

I celebrate your eyes
because they looked at me
without restraint
        and no shame.

I celebrate your breasts
in the darkest night
I could find them blind
        and feeble.

I celebrate your tears
even if they cry for something
        that I've done.

I celebrate you
playing shuffleboard
                    or tennis
or playing with my balls
while I'm asleep.

I celebrate
all the night sounds
that you make
but won't admit to,
your conversations
with yourself in sleep.

Most of all
I celebrate the god
that gave me you
and asked for nothing
in return.
He'll get a better man
one with more compassion
because he let me
stumble on to you.

## In Case You Didn't Know

Some days up ahead
will come down empty
and some years fuller
than the fullest ones
we've known before.

Today has been
the best day yet.
        I thought
you ought to know that.

And I thought it time
that I said *thank you*
for whatever might have
passed between us
that in your mind
you might have felt
missed my attention.

It didn't
and it doesn't
and it won't.

Thank you
for the everydays
that you make
into holidays.

I close up
more often now,
not just to you
but even to myself,
                within myself.

I know I should
be always open.
At least I ought to make
            a better try.

I will.

## Twelve

See the dog
he doesn't move—
      a voyeur.
Never mind.
What we've done is beautiful.
For gods and animals to see,
for us to stand aside
        in awe
  and look ourselves
        up and down.

Your breasts
are just your breasts,
        that's all,
but letting go to me
detaching from me
all the debts
I've paid that day—
smiles to secretaries mean
dividends to competition
                in my work,
courtesy to those
who'd break me down,
good morning
to the elevator man.

Your thighs
    make over all the scales
and so I hurry home
                    to you
to use your belly
            as a cape
to cover up the day.

## Second Weekend

I fly with you
between the covers
as easily as between
the clouds.

You transport me
            you carry me
loving you has made me
better than even God
could have expected.
Walk down a street with me.
Ride with me
past green hills
            to lower California.
It's as beautiful and open
            as flying free.

## Target Practice

I'm not sure
if I hit the target
or if the target turned,
aimed itself and fired at me.

We connected
in the New York winter,
over again and over again
proving that the aim
            was sure and true
or that adversaries can be
controlled, compounded and corraled
                        at will.

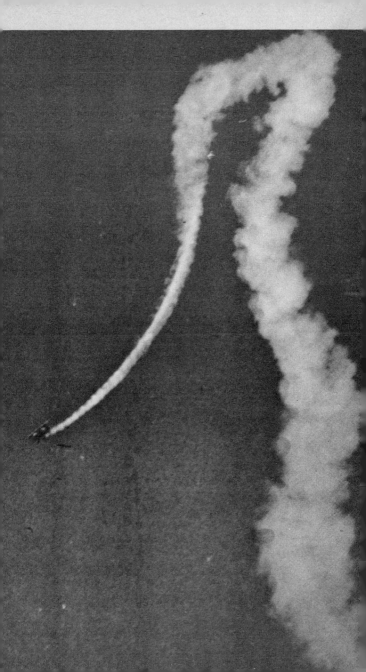

## Offering

Can I be of any help
with your suitcase
        or your trunk?
Can I stack the wood
against the door?
If your head's too heavy
let it fall against my arm.

Have you packages of love
that need untying
and tying up?
Let me first unfold
                your smile
and bend it to my own.

That's a beginning.

# Middle Mornings / Middle Nights

for Farol Seretean

The guarantee
for finding sanity again
is finding love again
and giving over
to the new beloved
that one facet of yourself
you held back last time.

—from *Moment to Moment*

## Midnight Saviour

Have you come
        to save me?
                Very well.

I'm teetering
between the earth
                and hell.
I'll gladly take salvation
over pot and pills
        and cheap red wine.
I'm grateful for your arms
but open up a little more
so that I need not love you
                    out of gratitude
but only for yourself.

Let me lie against
            your belly
inhaling all the night air
            you let out.

Let me
reach inside you
slow and easy
          deliberate
so that your anatomy
will be my primer,
your sighs now heavy
my own northeast wind.
          Let me probe
a secret place
no one else
has so far touched.

Allow me
this small favor
to pull you to me
from the inside,
to live inside you
half of every night
the star-filled half.

Don't be discouraged
if I fumble
or become inept.
I'll try again,
now slower still.

Then moving
        to your face
your eyes and hair
will dazzle me
as our mouths match,
the insides probing
one another's insides.

Slide next to me.
See,
no position
is uncomfortable
or wrong.

# Hotel Ansonia Poem

Now back into the pasture
two by two and hand in hand.
You are the science,
the surveyor of
the new survival route
if I am to come back home
with sanity or sense.

I no longer want
what I have never seen
a sometimes thing
forever out of reach.

How can I sigh and settle in
    for second best
when you have given me
both now and night.

What's left to me
           without you?
Flotsam maybe. Fodder,
        little more.
For I have fastened on
and am heading down
the new road.

I see no fences up ahead
no barriers or breakers
only fresh green turf
to chomp and stomp through.

Bruno at the beach is smiling.
Hermes waits within the town.
I care not
whether we sail out
          upon the ocean
or travel hills and gullies.
I only care
that you might not care
next week or next year.

Lock horns with me
or sleep beside me
while I'm wide awake
I'll teach you how
to go on caring
one more month,
another week,
an hour perhaps?

## Endangered Species

Once I wrote somewhere
*the eagle does not*
*hunt flies*
the words come back
to haunt me now.
I feel at once
  strong and *beautiful*
because you want me
yet apprehensive because
the rare birds
      fly so high
and I am only learning.

Will there be
enough time to catch up
to learn to soar
        on strange wings,
not merely flapping
            on my own?

We'll be together
by the week's end
and then make plans.

We'll go ballooning
        if you like,
that's part of my world
you've yet to see.
Or we'll spend another
        lengthy weekend
in my old/your new bed.

## Meeting

I admit that I am shy.
More so with those faces
and those forms
that I start to love
with but one look only.

Back in the room
we had no liquor
        and no radio
no aphrodisiac but need.
Oh, I needed you. I did, I do.

Your bushy head
and your big eyes,
your thighs
to wrap myself around,
your intermittent smile
                  and stare.
Your caring for me
then and now.

I pushed a pillow
soft beneath your head
and murmured love
from the beginning.

I knew. Don't ask how,
that we were starting
what could not be finished
          in our lifetimes.

Here we are
and those tomorrows
left or owed to me,
borrowed and as yet
              unbought for you
will not be enough.
We should move
towards the heavens
or at least above the earth
                somewhere
          for always.

Though I know
need is not enough
    perhaps this time
simple wanting
will transcend everything.
I always go straight forward
hoping that it will.

## Another Sunday

Save me one long Sunday
tucked away in your young life
rationed to me hourly,
if that has to be,
hired out to me at my own risk
not insured against
        time's accidents
and covered by no policy
except a deed of trust.

Save me one long Sunday
for the following and more:
One—to cycle silently
through some new park.
Two—to pencil in
the crossword of your living
(notice I said pencil,
knowing you're as changeable
and every bit as given
            to forgetfulness
                    as me).

Three—to bribe the bed
that it might stay unmade
and wide as Williamsburg,
through a day without beginning
                and no end.
Four—to hear you soft and steady
singing all the songs
I've never heard you sing before.

# Middle Night Confusion

As the sun has just now
bent down into the ocean,
          bend down to me.
Rising up
                    I promise
you'll not frown.

As the stars
begin appearing
move in closer
begin to pull me
                to you
as I pull you down.

As we roll sideways
see the path of moonlight
stretching on the water
wide enough to walk on
with an army
if one of us was God.

God is here somewhere
       between us.
I can touch and feel Him
lying up against
       your back,
one arm extended
through the roof
exchanging bulbs
in burnt-out stars.

But wait
there is no beach at all.
No moonlight on the water
no waves sing out to me.
Can this be so,
that in these hills
away from everything
          I knew before,
the only singing
                    my ears hear
is your sighs,
heavy, full of thunder?

One more time
and one more time again.
You are my ocean
        and my stars,
my God and all His heaven.
And life for me begins.

# *Apples*

for Helen Brann

The journey back
is longer than the forward run.

—from *Lonesome Cities*

## Apples

If you like apples
I'll carry home
        an orchard.
If sky is to your liking
I'll bundle up the skies
        of summer
so you'll never need to know
the winter evening anymore.

I like the fire
and so I wait
     for winter nights.
Apples I can take
         or leave

Your body
like your mind
has need of going over,
and I intend to be
a journeyman
of your soft skin
        for years.

## Declaration

Your mouth
is my undoing.

Closed or open,
                private
or in public places
I covet your mouth.
Often hearing not a word
that issues from it,
I still feel every breath
know each and every
                movement
                by heart.

Love, I do
and it's a new release,
one I should have
                come upon
a dozen years ago.
                I did.
It's only that we
                didn't know.

## Crosswalk

We touch,
shoulder-to-shoulder.
You can't do more
when crossing streets
with mannequins in windows
                looking back.

I try to match your step—
that way I'm sure
    of staying close.
You smell like love.
That must be so
  for what I smell
is dear to me and *new*.

And so a little walk
          through town
becomes a journey
a love vacation
          from ourselves
but with ourselves.
Everything you say
is funny or beautiful.

# The Rhythm of Spring

All the trees are pink.
Plum blossoms,
or are they small extensions
          of the clouds?
They fill the lower sky
     just above
the thin horizon
trapping the season
for all time.

Your smile
is one more opening
            into you
that I should
come  through softly.

Softly, I will come,
gentle I will be
concerning you.
Your rhythm
      will be my own.
Our heartbeats
should not be
      independent,
            but collective.

# Time Step

Before . . .
you
only
you
me
only
me
two
divided.

Now
we
are
one
together
till
time
swallows
itself.

# Footprints

Not content to fly
        to Cedar Falls
I'd like to track
the footprints on the moon
and come back home
with bouquets of spare junk.
So little mystery's left
in moon and moonlight
coming through the window
I'd like to bring back home to you
great handfuls of the Milky Way
to decorate your dressing table.

# A Number of Alternatives

You might have been a nun
           in love with God
thinking men not good enough
to see your close-cropped hair
or know your midnight eyes.

A drum majorette perhaps,
          with battered baton
who dreamed of Radio City
          on the football field.
Such a childhood
might have led you
to the silver screen
and not into my arms.

Women want
     the near impossible.
Knowing that,
the wise man stays ready.

We ask the difficult ourselves.
          Love us.
     For ourselves.

## Morning, One

It is the morning of our love
our sighs are all snow-silver white
and clean as breakfast napkins.

We'll go gently then
        into the day
keeping the morning in mind,
for too soon the sun
eats up the shadows.

Come see the pussy willows grow,
do up your hair and nothing else.
We'll buy up all the butterflies
        and make the morning last.

## Morning, Two

We sleep well together
in nobody's world
but our own.
            A Monday-sleep.
A stomach-to-stomach
                safety sleep,
that wraps us in each other
and takes us from ourselves.

The parish priest
worried over my soul
          when I was younger.
*We go to church one day a week*
*to take us from our selfish selves*
          he used to say.
It was the best excuse
                    I ever heard
for organized believing.

Who would have thought
religion was so simple?

## Lemon Leaves

You see how easily
we fit together,
as if God's own hand
        had cradled only us
and this beach town's population
                were but two,
this wide bed but a child's cradle
with room enough left over
                for presents.

Tomorrow I'll buy you presents.
Pomegranates and breadsticks,
tickets round the room and back
and red red roses
like everybody buys everybody.

Everybody's got a diamond ring
        and Sunday shoes.
Neckties and petticoats,
pistols and tennis balls.

What pleases you?
I'd hock my watch
to buy you Greece
or sell my car to bring you
rickshaws from Rangoon.

All they had
down at the corner
were poppies
with some lemon leaves.
They'll have to do
till I can bring home
                Union Square.

I found a twenty-dollar bill
            when I was ten.
I bought a cardboard circus
        and a fountain pen
and a jackknife
because I never had one before.
My mother thought
            I'd stolen the money.
I brought her perfume
        from the dime store.
            She believed me then.

I was rich in those days,
for a week I had everything.

I wish I'd known you then.

## Supper

All hills and gullies
mounds and little mountains
you rise up early
        in the night.
In dreams so real
that sleep and waking
meet, dissolve and blur.

A sacrament you are
        made of salt
and tasting not unlike
cinnamon or soda water
as I pull you to me.

A meal you are.
A meal you make of me.

We devour
one the other
as though we were
some hungry giants
having fasted
all the winter
hungry now for spring.

I see no end
to this stored-up appetite
          this emptiness
that only loving
up and down a lifetime
          will fill up.

I have wished too much
or just enough
          to bring you here
almost to the final step.

One meter gone
or one mile away
               you are
just out of reach
or too near
to make perspective work.

## Anthem #33

Bare-bellied
in the bedroom
or coming from the bath
you look like every invitation
to every party I dreamed of
that never came.

I salute the sensibility
of your stomach
and pledge allegiance to it
as my only flag.

I know
that I'm preoccupied
with backs and bellies,
I'm told that all the time—
but God's face and Syracuse
are too far out of reach
to be of any use at all.

## Contrast

I know love
by its first name
and living by its last.

I'm not afraid
of what's upcoming
or what has gone before
and if there's nothing left
to know about or learn
I'll review the early lessons
                    yet again.
But please
don't turn the light switch yet
as valuable and friendly
as the darkness is
leave the porch light on
                    for contrast.

# Moonraker

Dreams run to reality
and once or twice
the marriage works,
though in the end
reality dissolves
completely into dream.

—from *Come to Me in Silence*

## Art Instruction

Paint an owl
color in his wings
     and saucer eyes
gray feathers on the outside
white down just underneath.

Paint an owl
sitting on a single branch
throughout the night
hooting at the wind.

When you lay your brush down
                    afterward
you will have drawn
            or painted me.
Bewhiskered, living,
growing in the shade
of your so loved body.

Conjure up an owl
and you will have painted me
hunched up in the pillows
or squatting at the bed's edge
watching you in silent sleep.

## Shake and Bake

I owe you gratitude.
A multitude of thanks.
The kind of words
we never put to words
but hold as hostage
for some upcoming
all important time
when new words
must be summoned
to crowd the clichés out.

Restless I have been
like a sleek marauding cat
                pacing through
and racing through a night
when sleep not only didn't come
but stayed so far away
that I was surely posted
            as a vanguard
at the midnight's bedside.

For now I need to sleep.
Good morning
as you go to work.
Good evening
as you hurry home.

It isn't Rome or Tripoli
or even some beach place.
But this new bed will now attend
the deepest most untroubled sleep
a dozen days or half a decade's
                          brought me,
as I pretend
while getting drowsy
            you're still here.

And so when I wake up
            you will be.

## Down Under

Because I toured Down Under
my winter day was cut in half
and I survived two autumns.
Summer was not small enough
to hold, but it was small,
as all the days are little now
and every night is smaller still.

Now rain, now sun, now clouds
that jackknife in between.
But I'm not turned around
by seasons out of order
or made out of order
by seasons turned around,
for though the mileage
has been great
I've not moved at all.

## Timepiece

My watch still stays
on New South Wales time
and so I'm thirteen hours
up on all my friends.

I wonder
when I come to meet you
if I'll set my clocks and watches
to Pacific Standard Time.

Will I be living in the future
till I see you?
I seem to have
no need for now
for moving back
into the past.

It's three A.M.
in New South Wales.
If I were there
I'd fondle you
and jostle you awake.

Since I'm not
I watch the clock.
It moves so slowly
that I finally have to
                    turn away.
I'll write a letter
in the morning.
No, I'll start one now, today.

## Letter from Sydney

The letter finally came,
bushtail possum
          on the postage stamp
seven days from Sydney
                    to L.A.

No, six
moving past the dateline
          it came today.

I would that I
were traveling back
with your letter's answer
carried on my tongue
                    to yours.

I would look at you
in the easy winter night
of New South Wales
and you would know
my urgency for answers
        true and simple
not just luxury or need.
You are a fact for me
            not dream or fiction.

I agree that time
will test us
but time not spent with you
                is lost.

I so dedicate
what life I have
to you I love
and pray you spend it
                    generously
on what you love
and what you'll come
                    to love.

## Boundaries

I love you enough
to let you run
but far too much
to let you fly.

I'll let you walk
to the block's end
        by yourself
sail off on any lake
        or silent sea
but if I peer at you
as you go wandering
    through noisy rooms
know that I keep watch
for both of us.

I love you enough
to let you run
but far too much
to let you fly.

# The Lights Of London

for Peter and Tina
Friedlander,
from their children

I have no journey
that I care to make just now
unless it's to the middle of the bed.

—from *In Someone's Shadow*

# I Am Being Led Through Life

I love
with such a passion now
that death is imminent,
for what I love is easily
so true to me
that God would hardly
let me know
        the pleasure of it,
even one more day.
No man could have
                such happiness
and still be left to walk
this good green earth.

I so dedicate
what life I have
to you I love
and pray you spend it
                    generously
on what you love
and what you'll come
            to love.

Fields of wonder
are the places
God goes walking in,
I found them by mistake
and I've trespassed.

A mystic I am not
and yet I meditate again
amid the London morning
hoping that my thoughts
go back to California.
I cannot cable love
nor would I.
You must assume
        you must believe
that seven thousand miles
and more than seven hours'
                reach away
I am reaching out just now.

To the far fields I have gone,
down along the sea
above the hills and back again
thinking I was running
new ground all the time—
learning only now
that all those wondrous fields
are meadows that a new lifetime
would not last long enough
to take me through.

Never mind.

I've will enough to make
as many journeys as I can
in the name of love and longing,
and years to pay for time
                    I've wasted.

I am not sure
what waits beyond the block
but I'll travel down the street
                to have a look
        if need be.

Amen to what I knew before,
I thought that I was living.
No doors have opened up for me
and no new windows on the world
          only life itself.

I am being led through life
willingly and wide awake.
Your tongue has given birth to me
as surely as my mother
              thought she did.

# Monochrome/Portsmouth

A black kite
flying in the distance
farther down the beach
                then gone.
Black birds too are here
scavengering fish heads,
chasing off the killdeer
                and the gull.

The sea—
not blue but double grays,
goes on about its business.
It seems calmer now,
quieter today.

How long will it take,
another week perhaps
till every cloud above
                    the water
hangs there hidden, black.

The sand,
the stars, already dimming,
blackness in the end
will overtake them both.

How is it
people fear the dark?
Not me, I'm reconciled.
As every day I see
        the blackness grow,
I'm reconciled with black
it knows I know.

Yet I wonder
if the darkness
ever hungers
        or grows lonely
for the light
it's left behind.

## Brighton, 2

Today
you came toward me
            once again
as though we'd planned it.

Passing on, you smiled
as only beauty
has the charity to do.

Tonight then, in the bar
            I'll know you
by the back of your head
and the front of your smile.

You'll recognize me by my need.

That shouldn't worry you,
remember you looked first.
I'll admit I nearly stumbled
              looking back
but what a sight you were.

Tonight.
Though no plans
have yet been made
I'll be punctual
on time and on my mettle.

I come expecting nothing
(though secretly I know
that there is something
there has to be . . .).
Still whatever happens
is a gift of time
or touch or both.

## Twenty-nine

The spring has seen us both
side by side and singing.
Did you think I'd dare
to leave you walking lonesome
into someone else's summer?

If it's someone else you need
I'll take you to him
and find my way
back home alone.
But I'll not have you
going aimlessly away
whatever be your liking.

# Spring Song

Don't hurry spring
the wind still trembles
in the empty trees
and dead geraniums stand still
in Spanish Harlem window boxes.
Another week perhaps
when skaters leave the pond.

Now for a while longer
we can have the park
            to ourselves.

I need a while more with you
                    just now,
there are some things
I don't yet know.

Do you like the color blue
do I worry you when I frown
where were you
when I was growing up
and needed somebody?

## Boxing Lessons

Wiser by a half a year
I enter into your brown body
like a blind man
        sure of every step.
So assured
sometimes I feel embarrassed.

So delighted that I wonder
how I earned the privilege
of your light limbs
            around my back.

If indeed I've earned
your body and your love
then I'll return
        undefeated.

A man who by accident
           or even by design
who stumbled into something
so unusual yet real
he comes back smiling
like a sheepish child
from every new encounter
with your touch.

## Comfort

If we could do it
      all again
motorbike
   through Roman cities
in the rain
watch the cats chase lizards
          in the forum
and drink bad wine
from mouth to mouth
I probably would try
to love you harder than I did
I probably would smile a smile
much better than the ones
          you knew
for I was just rehearsing then
imagining what easily might happen
      in years to come.

It is not just you I love
(or even Roman rain)
or all the time you rattled
                    on my window
after twelve o'clock.

I love the smell of rooms—
where you have been
the foreign touch
of things I never knew
until you came along.

I even love your enemies
because they drive you
to my arms
            for comfort.

## Trust Me

Trust me
and I'll do
good things for you
even if to make you happy
means to leave you
to yourself.

## Highway, 22

Loving
is the only sure road
out of darkness,
the only serum known
that cures self-centeredness
or puts it there.

I have said I love your body
as I love my own.
I mean not just the contours
and the weight that shifts to me
but that I would protect you
from the robber baron
as I would protect myself.

## Camera

I stand *just so*.
Your camera winks me
    into permanence
acne scars
   tired eyes
wrinkles on my forehead
more naked than I have ever been
   (especially to one
    I love so very much).

I used to be afraid to look
     completely real
the sun was just my friend
       sometimes
when brown from sea and sky
   made things all right.

Always afraid
to be anything but young
and envying beauty
even on the face of strangers.

*Is this what growing up means*
the reality of lighting
          over public mirrors?
Or is my confidence in love
                    so great
that I worry not
to let you see me
          at my worst?

# *Intermission*

a pause is just
another kind of stop.

—from *With Love*

## Gentle Giants

Where have all
the gentle giants gone?
Don't they know
we need them now
If only just to lead us
through the winter night
and back again to spring?

# Definition

How to say *Love*
in a different way—
so seldom as to seem *new*
each time I say it
yet so often
        it reminds you
·of my obligation
and of yours,
to hold your hand
but not too tightly
to let you run
but not too far.

## People Riding Trains

People riding trains are nice
    they offer magazines
and chocolate-covered cherries,
the details you want most to know
about their recent operations.

If I'd been riding home to you
I could have listened
              with both ears
but I was on my way away.

Across from me
there was a girl crying
            (long, silent tears)
an old man held her hand.
It was only a while ago you said,
take the seat by the window,
                you'll see more.


                        This time
I filled the seat beside me
with my coat and books.
I'm antisocial without you.
I'm antiworld and people too.

Sometimes I think
I'll never ride a train again.
At least not away.

## The Middle and Both Ends

If you gave me children
            one or ten,
I couldn't love you more.
                Less maybe.
For I have only love enough
                for you.
It takes the middle
            and both ends
of all the love I've got
to keep you safe.

Children, then,
birds and trees
and summer afternoons
will have to be
my good friends only,
for I'm as selfish
          with my love
as you are with your body
in the morning.

## Furrows

Often I feel
the furrows on your forehead
are deep enough
to make a proper trench—
     and then you grin.

## In Passing

Yesterday,
did you remember
      how we met?

Today,
do you remember
      what I said?

Tomorrow,
will you remember
      how I tasted?
Some have said
I taste like almonds.

## December 9, 1976

I loom over you
for one long moment,
before I fall
to play and plunge and pillage.

Could I have been a pirate
in some other life?

If the heart
had been at prayer
I think I heard it
speak a word so softly
it must have meant amen.

## Exercise

You are/
you are not
with me.

Look close
and see you
looking back
as I look
back at you.

Interrupting
with a word
I know too well.

The word:
may be
*maybe* or
*unless*.

Conditions,
like a trial,
and I accept.
Don't go too far
(too far being
toward/away).

Jean Marc's top
is spinning
counterclockwise
from the corner
spider's web.

We reel, too.
Not, I fear,
as constant as a top.

The webs
we've made
and make
are tougher
than the spider's
and not as constant.

You are and
you are not
with me.
I accept.
I accept.

## Tuesday—Away

On this Tuesday
        away from you
I wonder if the time
            will ever pass
till we're together
even for a while again.

But yesterday you touched me
and we drove to the toll beach
and ran in the sand.
Sorry no one could see
how beautifully happy
            we were.

# Homecoming

**for the cats
in Clarendon Gardens**

I don't believe
that I was born
      to run
or that I'm happier
while on the move
      or going,
only that the need to go
occurs and reoccurs.

—from *Finding My Father*

## Nine Lives

Welcome home.
The cat remembers.
What kept you?
Never mind,
you're here.

## Atlantic and Pacific

Two cats adopted us
one black and white
the other white and black.

You never cared for cats,
            not really,
but I am ever grateful
that you indulged
my need for pastorale
that kitchen cats provide.

You silently forgave
their traipsing
        and trespassing
in and out of windows,
playing on the stairs
and drinking all the cream
                you'd hidden
for your morning coffee.

By that toleration
and your tales of Saki's Tobomoury
you spoke great volumes
of your love for me.

By your willingness
to learn about
and then be captured
        by a cat
you proved that even
after half a lifetime
of finding your own way
you still could help invent
a brand new common ground.

Two cats
one black and white,
another white and black.
No matter what
another book or bible says,
you have mastered shadings.
You know that grays exist.

Two cats.
The black and white one's
            called Atlantic
the white and black, Pacific.
Since both oceans
separate us far too often
I fantasize that when I'm gone
one or the other trods through
            Little Venice
and comes home to you
to lie contented through the night
        at our bed's end.

Two lives.
And whatever comes and goes
through the garden
                 or the window
they could not be closer
even at a distance.

Still for those minutes
once or twice a week
when doubt brought on by need
                 comes by,
leave the window open
so Atlantic and Pacific
can ebb and flow
in their natural course.

## What Is It?

Cloud formations
on a given day
and wondering
if you've seen them too
are enough to make a morning
                            pass for me.

Was your day
filled with wanting,
or the needlepoint of knowing
            that I waited
and that I wait for you?
I did.
I do.

Swing safely home to me,
              come evening.
Make room for me
within your life
and I'll make room for you
within my arms.

If you don't know algebra
or Alice by the fire,
or even why some roses
fail to climb the wall,
ask the question of me.
Never be afraid to say,
What is it?

# The Distance to Monterey

Silence is a better means
for telegraphing thought
than any Morse code
                    yet made.
I wonder if you know
how many conversations
we've been having
while no words passed.
I often think our silence
has energy enough
        to get us
all the way to Monterey
                    and back.

## No Whiskey Bars

The sky
is the forehead of the morning
passing the sun along the day,
distributing the clouds
that moved just overhead
and ride with us till nightfall.

And your eyes
are the bottom of the day
set on fire by words,
made to move by sighs
and the rustling of the trees.

We'll go to the hills then,
            take our time.
Climb until we find one
     closest to the sky.

I'll spread a blanket
          on the ground
and make a picnic of your body.
You'll face the sky
       and count the clouds
and when the counting stops
I'll take you home again,
down a dozen hills
under a hundred skies.

I know the ground is not yet
                green all over
but trust me.
I'll find the greenest hill of all
and your red dress
            will be the single flower
that grows against the grass.

Me and the day we care for you
without the rivalry
        of common lovers
and we'll be careful as the rain,
        gentle as the clouds.

# Hand Signals

**for Lawrence Butler**

What pawn shop of the mind
can index all those numbers
new people in the last four days
are all the ones that I remember.

—from *Stanyan Street & Other Sorrows*

# Colors and Changes

*Green* is not
as near as it might seem
*red* needs California to be seen
*gray* and *yellow* change
　　　　　and interchange.
But *blue's* a color
you can touch
or one that will touch you.

Some colors
in their hues
are only variations,
as some friends
                turn out to be
only shadows of each other.

## Bertha's Place

Come in
if you're a friend
       of Bertha's.

I am never sure anymore
if they are cruising me
or recognizing me.

Once a girl said
I remember you
you used to play
in them Roy Rogers movies.

I am not who you think I am
I replied.
My name is Truman Capote
and I was once President
of these United States.
Of course,
I should have said
Let's go home
I'll be who you want.

But I am only brilliant
when the chance has passed.

## Sleep After
## the Brighton Lanes

Saturday night
ducking, dodging
through the Brighton lanes,
pursuing and pursued.

When nothing comes
of conquest or conquistador
the quietude of that same
upstairs room
is like an iron mantle
clamping down and making
every organ useless.

And still sleep doesn't come.

It's then you know
that speech is nothing.
                    Not because
there is no one to speak to
but because yet one more time
you were not chosen
by the chosen
and you did not choose
                    to speak
even though the chosen
might have waited
thinking your words
should come out first.

Why do we study,
why do we become
        learned men?
Why do we cheat
            and force
and push our way
through what we think
are barricades,
when all the while
it is those same
blind barricades
and balustrades
that we're erecting?

When it comes to need
intellect could not be
             more useless
and there's not knowledge
near enough or deep enough
to satisfy or substitute.

With imagination so well worn
that a single sigh is every bit
as powerful as sublimation.

*Need* can drive you
down the darkest alley
and leave you beached and bloody,
waiting for the new encounter.

Need,
and need not gratified
has helped me understand
why the suicide can do it
and how the alcoholic can
transcend and thereby end
                his limit.

Monday morning,
out of step,
too little sleep
that came too late.
The car is waiting.
On to Bournemouth.

Another night of faces
not seen completely
        and not seen again.
There are eyes and forms
that stand out
        even in the dark.
They become then individuals
                not audience.
They never know
and I can't tell them.

What if I put the question
to some of those who linger
when the show shuts down
and the answer came back, *no?*

One more bed
in one more room
now sleep hurries in,
even though the senses
still stay poised
for the small
or great adventure.
                    Tomorrow
there's the London train,
a month to go
and then Los Angeles again.

## They

They are meeting in rooms
or turning in hallways.
They make covenants
in countries not known to me.
They poison the air
with their pride in each other.
They foul the night
with their gratified desires.

They muddle me
by passing past me
not noticing my need
pretending not to recognize
the hope that happens
              on my face
when one of them goes by.
They insult me
by insisting on each other.
They kill me with the care
they show their own.

They devour me by degrees
and I let them.

## Basic Training

Stumbling
    striding
  half running
down the stairs
to stand formation.

Awakened not by
just the cadre's whistle
or the threatened roll call
but mostly by
        the winter morning
hard against our faces.

Still buttoning shirts and
                    fumbling with flies,
our piss hard-ons now softened
by the cold October day
we stood the name count
                        squint-eyed,
not hearing anything
but one the other's
        stomach grumbling
asleep though standing
each anticipating his own name
and barking back affirmatively
                    when it came.

## Juan

I know the Spanish word
for yellow and for blue
and *rojas* is the name
                    for red
and why you run
and why I'm running too.

Have I passed the test
will you teach the rest
                to me
and grade my paper
            with affection
and some patience?

Can I count on you
to counsel me
and to let me counsel you?

I am asking
not for cake
or even bread
a shoulder and some beans
would more than fill
my small, but still important,
                    wants and needs.

## Baggage

The year was only
one long noisy day
that never knew
a quiet night.
           Your grin
(once strong as any shoulder)
                     disappearing
in so many crowded rooms
each time
I thought I'd found
your face again
hardly helped at all.

I suppose it was
a glad adventure
however quickly gone.
Still leave me
       your address
so I won't have to stand
                  in line
at American Express.

# Lee, the Summer's Over

Lee, wake up
the summer's over
we've got to make it
through another snowy year

Hang in there
and I'll take you through the clouds
the way you took me
bouncing down the weekend.

  Don't go yet
there's got
to be
some sea coast
we've not seen

Hold on to me
and we'll go flying
through the spring.

## Encounters

I'll ring up one day
and you may wonder
           who I am.

I too might not be sure
if you're the one
who smelled like violets
or left my shoulder
tattooed with a mark
that took three weeks
           to go away.

The one who,
going down the stairs,
turned  back
long enough to say
*Don't call me*
*after ten o'clock*
*my mother goes to bed*
              *quite early.*

Those of us who think
that *need* and *night*
are interchangeable
have so many scraps
                of paper
stuffed in wallets,
tucked up under books
or safely put away
        in dresser drawers.

Names and numbers
scribbled on the backs
of business cards
or finely printed
on torn matchbook covers.

I never have the guts
to throw them out.
Do you?

I suppose
that like a pilgrim
I keep imagining
my colony of cards
can one day be called up
to form a fort
against the need to walk.

I must remember
from now on to write
*thin shoulder blades*
or *this one had a mole*
*along the left side*
*of her underbelly.*
Some identifying thing
so if I ever make
            those calls
I'll know just who
            I'm calling.

I never make the calls
do you?

Yet still we think
the inside side
of matchbook covers
with a penciled number
is a kind of life insurance
that may bring about
a proper settlement
when the accident
of being with our own selves only
overtakes us in an alleyway
                    or bedroom.

# Looking Ahead

**for Mark Rosenfeld**

now becomes
tomorrow
with the lateness
  of the hour.

  —from *Moment to Moment*

## Front Runner

The lifetime I have left
I open up to you
to tread upon
and travel through.

You pave the road
        I'll follow,
you build the bridge
        I'll test it first.

## Write Me a Poem

Write me a poem.
Make me a song.
Tell me a story
I don't yet know.
Speak to me slowly
of fire and Friday
and tell me how nice it is
                          walking alone.

Not reassurance
but reason I need
for Spring's at the window
slowing the day down.

So write me a poem
using few words
my span of attention
is five lines, no more.

## Absolutes

How true is truth
       how absolute?
If I say love
do I mean loving you
to the exclusion of all else
and of all others?
And do I know
if I mean that?

There are wild roses
that have bloomed
        far into December,
seemingly without a reason.
And some faithful trees
stay barren all year long.
Proving, I suppose,
the only thing consistent
        is inconsistency.

Let me say
I will not lie to you
and know I'm lying.
Nor will I comfort you
in any false way
however expedient that may seem.

And if I catch myself pretending
I'll tell on me
however much it hurts.

Fall down
with me, for now
and let me prove to you
how much I love
inside out and outside in.
If you're still afraid
then guide me if you like.
I love your hand
as much as I love
what's inside your heart.

## Atlantic Crossing

I gave up airplane praying
                a while back.
I'd done the yellow beaches
                and the bars.
Written songs enough
to keep my family safe for years.
Had some women
that I liked and learned from,
some I didn't.

My animals
could live in luxury
I'd miss them more
than they'd miss me,
but they'd be taken care of.
So if it came for me
the way it did for Doug
there wouldn't be much left
                          undone.

I'd have painted
almost every picture
that I started out to paint.

I'll admit
there were some
            eyes I'd caught
that I'd have liked to keep.
But all in all I felt
        that I was ready
so I didn't pray on airplanes
                    anymore.

God hadn't frightened me
                for years
the way He first did
when I'd run down
        his private fields.

We'd done some playing
in the sky together
and if we weren't
            on equal terms
I felt we had respect
for one the other.

Then you came running in my life.
                    I grew an inch.
And now while coming home to you
I go on praying
till the seat belt sign
                  goes off
            and then I pray again.

God let me live another day
to see you framed in any doorway
                  one more morning.

Don't let it happen
on an airplane ride
when for that instant
while I look at death
I might by chance forget
the color of your eyes.

# Running in Place

Often I wonder
why we go on running.
There are
so few things pretty
left in life to see.

That is until tomorrow
when the crocus jumps up
back in California courtyards,
and you become
my back rest
and my English Bible.

I don't believe
that I was born
        to run
or that I'm happier
while on the move
        or going,
only that the need
to be off and gone
occurs and reoccurs.

I'm not sure
that I'd stop still
        if I could,
or find a place
        and stay there.

But I have run
and I have flown
Always away,
never *to* anything
and I am not sure
the running has as yet
        or will ever
            stop.

There would always be
one more road ahead
one path not found
that should be.
Some place off beyond
some hidden bend,
better than
the bend before.

*End Papers*  **for Kathleen in Ft. Lauderdale**

Silence is the science of the times that stay. And yet we use whole paragraphs to say what saying nothing could have spoken better.

—from *Come to Me in Silence*

## Dinosaurs

A string untied
needs tying up
as every empty space,
to merely prove
its own existence,
needs walking through.

While mystery is a mainstay
the lack of knowledge
on a chosen subject
needs the miner's pick
the mason's trowel
and the astronomer's
strict surveyor's gaze.

Dinosaurs
once walked the earth
                but where?
I haven't been there.

How many comets
        have I charted
as they arched across
the winter sky, then fell?
None has fallen
near enough for me to see
the well it dug on impact.

If I traveled
every hour of every day
through the second half
of my own lifetime
there would still be spaces
I'd have liked to fill
if only for an hour.

Some things demand
a finding out
as some loose strings
          need tying
and so a map is brought out
x'ed and circled and gone over.

# Hand in Hand in Hand

Where once the wind
could blow me down
it seldom shakes me now
and no rain falling interferes
with sleep or my digestion.

Age, perhaps, or letting go

I only know it's easier these days
to move from bed to bathroom,
                              back again
and down the kitchen stairs.

I travel hand in hand
         with something
that is or is not there.

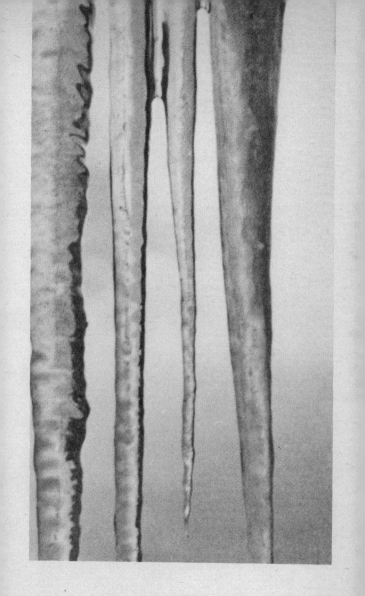

# About The Author

This is the third collection of Rod McKuen's poetry to be published by Pocket Books. The previous titles were *Seasons in the Sun* and *Alone*. Later this year Berkley will publish the author's hardcover best seller, *Finding My Father,* in paperback.

Rod McKuen's books of poetry have sold in excess of 16,000,000 copies in hardcover, making him the best-selling and most widely read poet of our times. In addition, he is the best-selling living author published in hardcover today. His poetry is taught and studied in high schools, colleges, universities, and seminaries throughout the world.

Mr. McKuen is the composer of more than 1,500 songs, which have been translated into Spanish, French, Dutch, German, Russian, Japanese, Czechoslovakian, Chinese, Norwegian, Afrikaans, and Italian, among other languages. They account for the sale of more than 180,000,000 records. His songs include "Jean," "Love's Been Good to Me," "The Importance of the Rose," "Rock Gently," "Ally Ally, Oxen Free," and several dozen songs with French composer Jacques Brel, including "If You Go Away," "Come Jef," "Port of Amsterdam," and "Seasons in the Sun." Both writers term their writing habits together as three distinct methods: collaboration, adaptation, and translation.

Mr. McKuen's film music has twice been nominated for motion picture Academy Awards (*The Prime of Miss Jean Brodie* and *A Boy Named Charlie Brown*). His classical music, including symphonies, concertos, piano sonatas, and his very popular *Adagio for Harp & Strings,* is performed by leading orchestras. In May, 1972, the London Royal Philharmonic premiered his *Concerto No. 3 for Piano & Orchestra,* and a suite, *The Plains of My Country.* In 1973 the Louisville Orchestra commissioned Mr. McKuen to compose a suite for orchestra and narrator, entitled *The City.* It was premiered in Louisville and Danville, Kentucky, in October of that year, and was subsequently nominated for a Pulitzer Prize in music.

In July, 1976, two new McKuen works were premiered at St. Giles Church, Tripplegate, in the old city of London: a Concerto for Cello and Orchestra, and the first major symphonic composition written for Synthesizer & Symphony Orchestra (*Concerto for Balloon & Orchestra*). He has been given a new commission by the city of Portsmouth, England, for a symphonic work to commemorate the sailing of the first ships from that city to Australia. The new work will be jointly premiered in Portsmouth and Australia's Sydney Opera House. Mr. McKuen was the first American artist to perform a series of concerts during the opera house's opening season.

Before becoming a best-selling author and composer, Mr. McKuen worked as a laborer, radio disc jockey, and newspaper columnist, among a dozen other occupations. He spent two years in the army during and after the Korean War.

Rod McKuen makes his home in California in a rambling Spanish house, which he shares with a menagerie of Old English sheep dogs and a dozen cats. He likes outdoor sports and driving and has recently started taking flying lessons.

As a balloonist, he has flown in the skies above the western United States and recently South Africa.

The author has just completed the libretto and music for a full-length opera, *The Black Eagle*. A new book of poetry, *The Sea Around Me . . . The Hills Above,* has recently been published by Hamish Hamilton in Great Britain. It is the first part of a projected trilogy; the second part, *Coming Close to the Earth,* will be published in the fall of 1977.

Much of Mr. McKuen's time is now spent working with his nonprofit foundations, Animal Concern and Basta. He has resumed concert activities, having taken a year's sabbatical to write his first novel, a lengthy work, as yet untitled, that spans three decades.

# DELUXE ROD McKUEN 2 RECORD SETS... ONLY $3.00 EACH.

**2SR 5051**
**ROD McKUEN**
**THE AMSTERDAM CONCERT**

Kaleidoscope/On the Road Again/
As I Love My Own/I'll Catch The
Sun/Jean/So My Sheep May
Safely Graze/The Dog and Me/
Children One and All/Hit 'Em In
The Head With Love/Love's Been
Good to Me/The World I Used to
Know/ If You Go Away/Spoken
Intro & I'm Not Afraid/Soldiers
Playoff/The Importance of the
Rose/Three/When Winter Comes/
Thursday/And So Goodbye/The
Complete Madame Butterfly/Bon
Soir Mademoiselle/Seasons in the
Sun/Without a Worry in the
World/Joe Smith is in a Meeting/
Soldiers Who Want to be Heroes/
Amsterdam/Soldiers Walkoff
Intro & And to Each Season/
Closing Remarks & Soldiers
Walkoff

**2SR 5092**
**ROD: 1957-1977**
What I Did For Love/Head Like A
Rock/Send In The Clowns/Jaws/
An Isle On The Water/Goodbye/
It Was A Very Good Year. Nearly
thirty selections featuring Rod and
guest artists Petula Clark, Lionel
Hampton, David Gates, Glen
Campbell, Roy Clark, Barry
McGuire and others. A thoroughly
unique album. From poetry to folk,
from disco to classical.

**2SR 5048**
**ROD McKUEN**
**LISTEN TO THE WARM**

All the titles from the original
best-selling album plus 14 tracks
never before recorded or released
—all from Rod's most popular
book of poetry.

**2WS 1894**
**ROD McKUEN/PASTORALE**

Fields Of Wonder/Pastorale.
Part 1/Make It With You/Three/
Something/He Ain't Heavy. He's
My Brother/I Think of You/Long.
Long Time/Before the Monkeys
Came/Kill the Wind/Nothin's
Gonna Change My World
and 14 more!

**2SR 10002**
**McKUEN MUSIC**
A Man Alone/Through European
Windows/Love's Been Good To
Me/ The Lovers/Gone With The
Cowboys/The Lonely Things/
Blessings In Shades Of Green/
The Loner/Jean/A Cat Named
Sloopy/Channing Way/Some
Trust In Chariots/The Single Man/
So Many Others/So Long, San
Francisco/Bend Down And Touch
Me/Alamo Junction/Love, Let
Me Not Hunger/Rock Gently/
Meantime/Listen To The Warm/
The Beautiful Strangers/Kaleido-
scope/As I Love My Own/Happy
Birthday To Me/Where Are We
Now?/Lloyd's Room/Hit 'Em In
The Head With Love/A While More
With You/Empty Is/ and more.

# SPECIAL DOUBLE RECORD OFFER

The publishers of this book and the staff of Stanyan Records thank you for your interest in Rod McKuen and invite you to take advantage of a very Special Rod McKuen record offer. You may select any *one* of five beautiful two-record sets for only $3.00, including postage and handling:

THE AMSTERDAM CONCERT. An unforgettable collection recorded live before an audience that gave the singer/performer a ten minute ovation. Two discs that readily tell why "The London Times" terms McKuen "one of the great entertainers of this generation . . . the best America has to offer."

LISTEN TO THE WARM. Now at last the two-record set. A gold record based on one of Rod McKuen's best-loved books. Poetry, songs, and beautiful backing by the Stanyan Strings.

PASTORALE. An unusual concept album that contains some of Rod's best songs and others written by Lennon & McCartney, David Gates, Petula Clark.

McKUEN MUSIC. A full symphony orchestra plays sixty of the composer's most enduring songs. Lush *foreground* music.

ROD: 1957-1977. Brand new. Songs, poetry, classical and film music . . . every phase of McKuen's twenty year recording career. Nearly thirty selections never before collected together — many previously unreleased. The surprise record of the year with guest appearances by other artists.

— — — — — **ORDER BLANK** — — — — — —

☐ ROD McKUEN/PASTORALE   ☐ LISTEN TO THE WARM
☐ McKUEN MUSIC   ☐ ROD: 1957-1977
☐ THE AMSTERDAM CONCERT

Please mark the album you would like (and alternate choice). Send this coupon together with a check or money order to: CHEVAL/STANYAN CO., 8440 Santa Monica Blvd., Los Angeles, Ca. 90069, U.S.A. Note: Canadian residents send 50¢ extra. Sorry no C.O.D.s.

Name_____

Address_____

City_____ State_____ Zip_____

Note: Only one album per order . . . please make alternate choice.

# Sources

"Endangered Species," "Monochrome/Portsmouth," "Meeting," "Midnight Saviour," "December 9, 1976," "Middle Night Confusion," "Shake and Bake," "Hotel Ansonia Poem," and "Atlantic and Pacific" are from *The Sea Trilogy,* which consists of *Coming Close to the Earth, Touching the Sky,* and *The Sea Around Me . . . The Hills Above.* All three volumes will be published in Great Britain by Hamish Hamilton/Elm Tree Books before making their appearance in the United States. *The Sea Around Me* was published in September, 1976, to be followed by *Coming Close to the Earth* in August, 1977.

Additional poems that have not appeared in any of the author's books in this country include "Hand in Hand in Hand," "Definition," "Nine Lives," "Colors and Changes," "Contrast," "Target Practice" and "Boundaries."

"Art Instruction" is from *Omnibus,* also available only in Great Britain.

"Running in Place" and "Dinosaurs" are part of the author's first book of published prose, *Finding My Father.*

"Atlas," "Apples," Declaration," "Footprints," "Boxing Lessons," "Furrows," "In Passing," and "The Distance to Monterey" appeared in *With Love*.

"Creed," "Spaces," "Another Sunday," "Down Under," "Exercise," "February Morning, 2," "Gentle Giants," "Lee, the Summer's Over," "Second Weekend," "Supper," and "Write Me a Poem" are from the *Animal Concern Calendar and Datebook*.

"Time Step" is from *And Autumn Came*.

"Morning, One," "Morning, Two," "Atlantic Crossing," and "Baggage" are from *Lonesome Cities*.

"Anthem #33," "Trust Me," "Highway, 22," "Front Runner," and "Twenty-Nine" are from *Caught in the Quiet*.

"Brighton, 2," "Juan," and "Timepiece" are from *Beyond the Boardwalk*.

"Spring Song," "Comfort," and "Camera" are from *Stanyan Street & Other Sorrows*.

"The Middle and Both Ends," "No Whiskey Bars," and "Encounters" are from *In Someone's Shadow*.

"Sleep After the Brighton Lanes" is from *And to Each Season*.

"Absolutes" and "Invocation" are from *Come to Me in Silence*.

"Exercise," "Worry," and "In Case You Didn't Know" were published in *Moment to Moment*.

"Bertha's place," "Excelsior," "Letter from Sydney," and "Rhythm of Spring" are from *Celebrations of the Heart*.

"Twelve," "Crosswalk," "A Number of Alternatives," "Lemon Leaves," "People Riding Trains," and "Tuesday—Away" were first published in *Listen to the Warm*.

"Offering" is from *The Carols of Christmas*.

"I Am Being Led Through Life," "What Is It?," "They," and "Basic Training" are from *Fields of Wonder*.

---

Sources for the part-title page couplets are as follows: Preamble—*Beyond the Boardwalk*; Two by Two—*Beyond the Boardwalk;* Middle Mornings—Middle Nights—*Moment to Moment*; Apples—*Lonesome Cities*; Moonraker—*Come to Me in Silence*; The Lights of London—*In Someone's Shadow;* Intermission—*With Love*; Homecoming—*Finding My Father*; Hand Signals—*Stanyan Street & Other Sorrows*; Looking Ahead—*Moment to Moment*; End papers—*Come to Me in Silence*.

# Index To First Lines